W9-ACH-288

# WHAT DO THEY DO?
# DENTISTS

## BY GAETANO CAPICI

**CHERRY LAKE** Publishing

Published in the United States of America by Cherry Lake Publishing
Ann Arbor, Michigan
www.cherrylakepublishing.com

Content Adviser: Grace Yum, DDS, Pediatric Dentist, Yummy Dental for Kids
Reading Adviser: Cecilia Minden-Cupp, PhD, Literacy Consultant

Photo Credits: Cover and page 1, ©Yuri Shirokov, used under license from Shutterstock,
Inc.; page 5, ©iStockphoto.com/monkeybusinessimages; pages 7, 15, and 17, ©Denise
Mondloch; page 9, ©iStockphoto.com/LeggNet; page 11, ©iStockphoto.com/nyul; page 13,
©iStockphoto.com/fishwork; page 19, ©iStockphoto.com/jacomstephens; page 21,
©iStockphoto.com/Philary

**LIBRARY OF CONGRESS CATALOGING-IN-PUBLICATION DATA**
Capici, Gaetano, 1985–
  What do they do? Dentists / by Gaetano Capici.
    p. cm.—(Community connections)
  Includes bibliographical references and index.
  ISBN-13: 978-1-60279-806-9 (lib. bdg.)
  ISBN-10: 1-60279-806-0 (lib. bdg.)
  1. Dentistry—Juvenile literature. 2. Teeth—Care and hygiene—Juvenile
literature. I. Title. II. Title: Dentists.
  RK63.C37 2011
  617.6'45—dc22                              2009042802

Cherry Lake Publishing would like to acknowledge the
work of The Partnership for 21st Century Skills. Please
visit *www.21stcenturyskills.org* for more information.

Printed in the United States of America
Corporate Graphics Inc.
July 2010
CLFA07

DENTISTS

# CONTENTS

WHAT DO THEY DO?

# SOMETHING TO SMILE ABOUT

"Ready?" asks the woman behind the camera. You flash a big, bright smile. Click! She snaps a picture of your class. You work hard to keep your smile looking great. You brush your teeth and **floss** each day. Who else helps you with those beautiful teeth? The dentist does!

Your dentist helps keep your smile looking great.

Dentists are special doctors. They keep our teeth and **gums** in top shape. Many dentists have important helpers. Some helpers are **dental assistants**.

Dental assistants get you ready to see the dentist. They may take **X-rays** of your teeth. Assistants also hand tools to the dentist as she works on your teeth.

When you get an X-ray, a dental assistant helps put the machine in place.

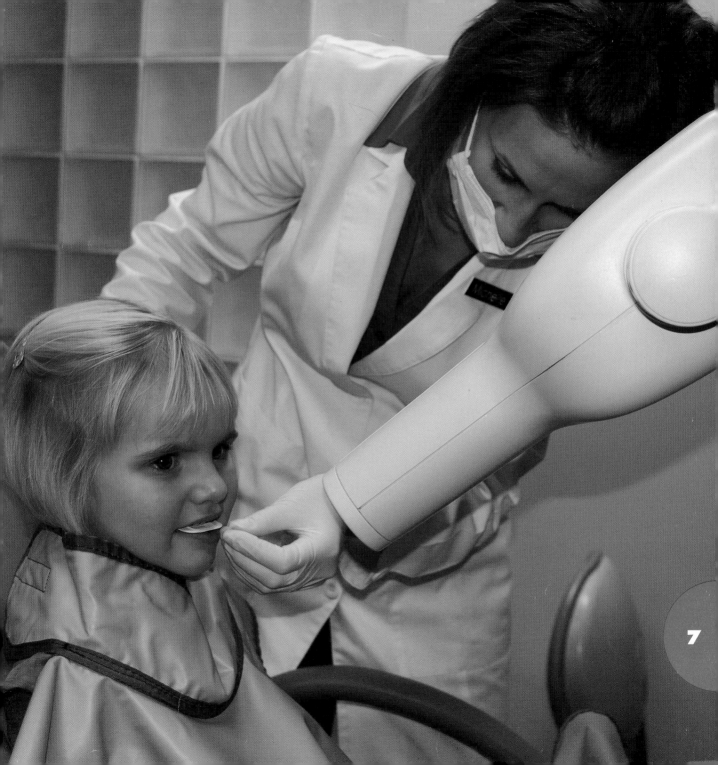

Other helpers are **dental hygienists**. They clean your teeth and gums. They use special tools to remove **plaque**. Plaque is a sticky coating that forms on teeth. It is made of germs. It can harm your teeth and gums.

Hygienists use dental floss to clean between your teeth. They treat your teeth with **fluoride**. They also polish teeth with a special paste.

A dental hygienist cleans your teeth with special tools.

People wear special items when they work on your teeth. They cover their mouths and noses with masks. They wear safety glasses and gloves, too. Why do you think that is? Hint: Think about germs and how they can spread.

# OPEN WIDE!

The dentist checks your teeth after they are clean. He looks for any problems. Dentists use a special tool called an **explorer**. It helps the dentist feel every part of your teeth. A tiny mirror helps the dentist see behind your teeth. He carefully checks for **cavities**. Cavities are holes in your teeth.

A dentist checks your teeth for cavities and other problems.

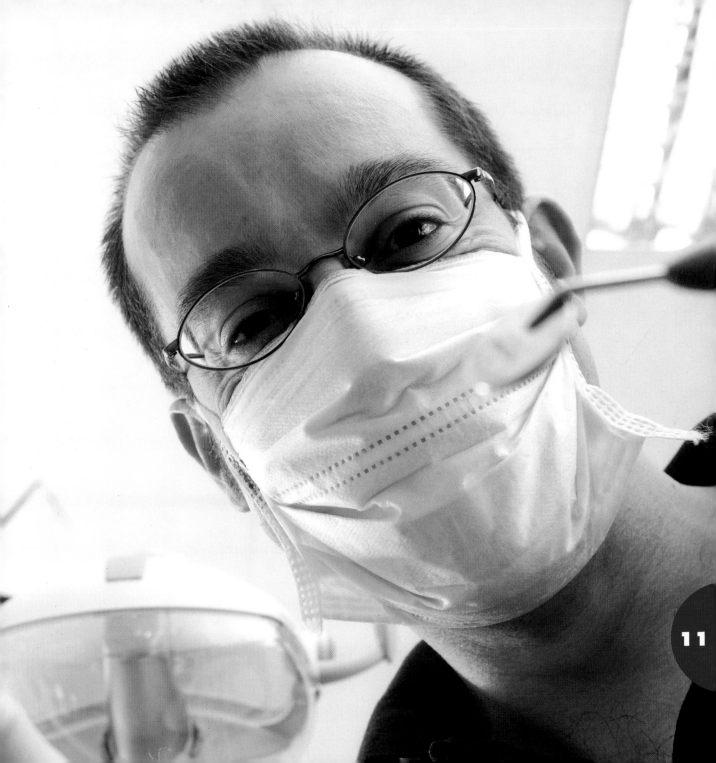

Sometimes, food sticks to your teeth when you eat. The germs in plaque feed on sugar in food. This can eat away at your teeth. Then you get cavities.

Sugary treats can lead to cavities. Healthy snacks, such as apples, are better for your teeth.

Many dentists never stop learning. They keep up with new ideas. They learn about better ways to care for our mouths. Has your dentist learned something new about teeth lately? Ask! She'll be glad that you want to learn more, too.

13

A dentist studies the X-rays of your teeth. This helps him see the parts of your teeth under the gums. X-rays also help dentists find hidden cavities. What if the dentist spots a cavity?

He uses tools to clean out the cavity. Then he puts in a **filling**. The filling is made of plastic or metal. It protects your tooth.

A dentist looks at X-rays of your teeth.

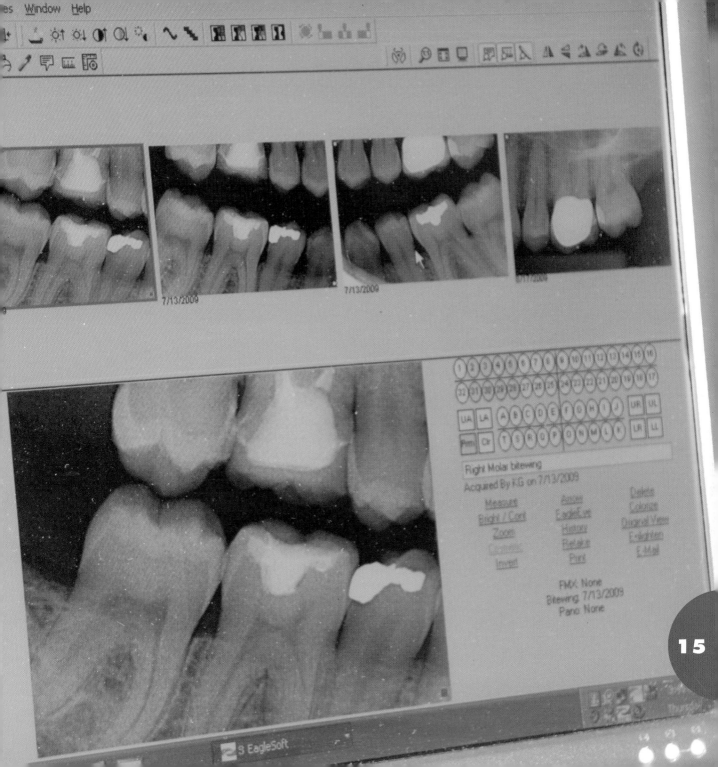

Dentists take care of your teeth in many ways. Sometimes dentists **extract** teeth that cannot be fixed or saved. Some dentists treat the gums or bones in the mouth. Dentists also give you great tips. They explain which foods harm your teeth. They show you the right way to brush and floss.

Dentists and hygienists can help you learn to brush and floss correctly.

Adults sometimes lose their teeth. Special dentists make fake teeth to replace them. Other special dentists straighten teeth that are crooked. There are also dentists who teach other people to become dentists. Other kinds of dentists come up with new ways to take care of teeth.

Some dentists can give you braces for crooked teeth.

People study for a long time to become dentists. How many years do you think they go to school? Make a guess. Now find the answer. Library books about dentists are one place to look. So is the Internet. Was your guess close?

# TIP-TOP TEETH

Are you visiting the dentist soon? She works to keep your mouth healthy. You can help make her job easier. Take good care of your teeth. Be sure to brush and floss every day. You can look forward to more than just great class pictures. You can have healthy teeth for the rest of your life!

Brushing is one great way to take care of your teeth.

# GLOSSARY

**cavities** (KAV-uh-teez) hollow spaces or holes in teeth

**dental assistants** (DEN-tuhl uh-SISS-tuhntss) people who help dentists as they work

**dental hygienists** (DEN-tuhl hye-JEH-nistss) people who clean teeth using special tools

**explorer** (ek-SPLOR-ur) a long metal tool that dentists use

**extract** (ek-STRAKT) to take or pull out something

**filling** (FIL-ing) material that is put in a tooth to fix a cavity

**floss** (FLAWSS) to clean between teeth with special string

**fluoride** (FLAWR-ide) a chemical combination that is put in water and toothpaste to prevent tooth decay

**gums** (GUHMZ) smooth, pink flesh that surrounds the base of teeth

**plaque** (PLAK) a sticky layer that forms on teeth

**X-rays** (EKS-rayz) special pictures that show parts of the teeth or body that cannot be seen from the outside

# FIND OUT MORE

## BOOKS

Miller, Edward. *The Tooth Book: A Guide to Healthy Teeth and Gums.* New York: Holiday House, 2008.

Ziefert, Harriet. *ABC Dentist.* Maplewood, NJ: Blue Apple Books, 2008.

## WEB SITES

### American Dental Association—Visit the Dentist with Marty
*www.ada.org/public/games/marty.asp*
Follow along as a boy visits the dentist in this fun, interactive story.

### KidsHealth—Going to the Dentist
*kidshealth.org/kid/feel_better/people/go_dentist.html*
Learn more about what dentists do, and what to expect when you visit one.

# INDEX

24

## ABOUT THE AUTHOR

Gaetano Capici graduated from DePaul University with bachelor's degrees in English and Spanish. He lives near Chicago, Illinois. He thanks his dentist for keeping his teeth clean and healthy.